MACRAME:

A beginner's guide to learn macramé and easy
modern patterns and projects

Madeline Stitch

TABLE OF CONTENTS

Introduction

When it comes to finding a creative hobby where you could make useful items—such as jewelry and home décor, Macramé is on top of the list.

Macramé is known as a form of knotting to create textile, instead of making use of knitting and weaving. It originated back in the 13th century, when Arabic weavers made use of the word "Migramah" to call what they had been making. This was because they resembled fringes, and in time, Turkish weavers also made use of the hobby, and called it "Makrama"—or the art of weaving excess pieces of fabric together.

Whatever its history is, one thing is for sure: Macramé is one of the best things you could do with your time. And, with the help of this book, you'll learn how to make various jewelry and home décor using the Macramé technique—and of course, you'll learn some Macramé background, too!

Macramé is defined as the art of knotting string in a decorative pattern. It is a French word meaning knot and is believed to be one of the oldest forms of art. Macramé is done by hand, without needles or a machine. The patterns are made by intricate tying ad knotting string in a particular manner to achieve the knot you are after. There are a number of different knots however the most common is the square knot and the half knot. These knots help create borers and braids that work into the Macramé art. There are over 50 different types of Macramé knots.

The knots in Macramé can be classified broadly into Basic knots and Vintage knots. Basic knots are simple, less elaborate and are ideal for beginners. The basic knots can easily be learnt and can be used to create simple repeating patterns. Vintage knots, on the other hand are usually more intricate, and require practice and skill to execute successfully. Vintage knots usually have an interesting historic significance, and with them, you can create items that help you imagine how decorative articles looked millennia ago. Popular vintage knots include Chinese knots and Celtic knots. Macramé looks amazing when used in bracelets, and describes your look. It also makes a statement about your preference of fashion accessories, as it is common knowledge that beautifully designed handmade jewelry is always done. This classic rope braiding is typically used to hold beads and gemstones firmly and nicely together. It is versatile, flexible and can be tailored to many items. Macramé's versatility makes it the perfect match for the colorful gemstones and other beads which make the bracelets charming. Chinese knots, as the name depicts can be traced back to ancient China, and some of these vintage knots date back as far as 2000 years. Several people over time, have invented newer kinds of knots to produce unique designs. Celtic knots, on the other hand, are even more rare and detailed. Celtic knots are better suited for extremely elaborated hand-crafted jewelry and fashion accessories.

So, now that we've examined the importance and significance of Macramé's numerous knots, it is time for us to get to the nitty-gritty of how to make these knots and start working on our personal Macramé projects.

Chapter 1 Story Of The Macramé

What is Macramé?

Macramé as an aspect of decorative knots permeates nearly every culture, but within those cultures, it can manifest in different directions. The carefully braided strings, with the assistance of a needle-like tool, became the item for shaping fishnets. Their use in the fashion industry has been spectacular and influential among the youth in making sandals, shoes, jewelry, etc. It is now used also with other products to fashion all kinds of beautiful works of art.

Macramé is a kind of fabric which is produced using methods of knotting (as opposed to weaving). The first knots of macramé are the square (or knot of coral reef) and "hitching" forms: various combinations of fifty per cent hitches. These are soon designed by sailors to cover anything from knife dealings with containers to parts of ships, particularly infancy or ornamental kinds of knotting.

Reverse fifty percent hitches are sometimes made use of to preserve equilibrium when working left and also right fifty percent of a balanced item.

Natural leather or fabric belts are an additional device commonly created through macramé methods. A lot of friendship armbands traded among schoolchildren, and also teenagers are developed utilizing this approach.

Suppliers at amusement parks, shopping malls, seasonal fairs, as well as various other public places may sell macramé jewelry or design as well.

The fundamental principle that includes jobs such as plant wall mounts and also owls. With a collection of blogs, I wish to present the knotting techniques, as well as start off with some simple tasks which I will create for you. We will certainly start with a description of the materials we will certainly utilize and also where they can be bought.

There are numerous sorts of cord utilized in macramé. Natural cables consist of jute and hemp. There is an all-natural charm to these cords, as well as they may be substituted in any of the tasks I show to you. My choice is to use just a synthetic rope, which is constructed from the herculean fiber. These cords are washable, as well as can likewise be cleaned and warm-fused. They are additionally discolored proof.

Cords are readily available in differing density varying from .5 to 8mm primarily; the larger the number, the thicker the cable, so 8mm is the thickest. We will, additionally, be using metal rings and beads. The most convenient way to work a job is on a level macramé board. The piece is held in the area, making use of t-pins, which assist with the spacing of knots in the patterns.

Hobby Lobby is a great area to grab vital supplies. They bring an excellent option for rings. They also have an appropriate selection of grains. They offer synthetic cord in 2 mm, 4 mm, as well as 6 mm, which are the densities I will certainly be using. Macramé boards are offered at Amazon.com, and both resources I will undoubtedly follow. Pepperell Braiding and also Kings Country are both sources online with the very best option. You can buy cord in numerous shades, including steel, Marbella, as well as bamboo rings, beads of all kinds, and macramé boards. It is best to save these places for bigger orders because of delivery costs.

Macramé is an approach to producing fabrics that use knots rather than weaving or knitting methods. Macramé was often utilized by seafarers to embellish products or their ships as well, as is additionally made use of to develop jewelry, bags, mats, plant hangers, and wall surface hangings. Occasionally, natural leather and also suede are used to produce macramé belts, as well as the relationship armbands made by several children, are produced utilizing macramé.

There is a big series of knots as well as knot mixes utilized in macramé consisting of the square knot, fifty percent knot, fifty percent hitch, larks head knot, and also coil knot. Depending on the knots used, as well as whether they are used alone or combined with others, several layouts can be accomplished.

The Macramé Is Back

The macramé technique was trending in the 1960s and 1970s. There are people who still keep magazines, clothing and decorative accessories made with macramé during the Happier. People who wore clothes or accessories made with macramé at this time were considered at reredos vanguards.

That is why the magazines that some people keep from Macramé are from those years, period of significant changes in culture, music, film and television. Indeed, I would need another book to talk about the changes that have occurred during these years.

For some reason, the macramé fell asleep to wake up in this new era of Instagram, Pinterest, Facebook and other social networks that invade us with images and trends. As we already know, fashion always comes back. However, I hope that this passthrough the knots are more than just a passing fad. I hope you stay to continue designing, dreaming and creating.

Times change, the world evolves and you always have to move forward, face them and grow with them. Now we have social media; in a few years it will be something else. For now, I enjoy this new stage in my life writing this book for you, which you read to me. For you who enjoy this new opportunity that we are giving to the macramé... as much as I do.

Macramé History

Macramé is considered, to begin with, Arab weavers from the 13th century. These artisans have knotted the excess film and yarn on the edges of hand-held towels, scarves and veils into decorative fringes. The Spanish word macramé derives from the Arabic migramas (Courtesy of the Common Chemicals), supposed to mean "striped robe," "ornamental fringe" (ornamental fringe) or "embroidered veil."

Macramé 's roots are the art of joining knots to shape beautifully laid out textiles. Many people claim that the term macramé originates from the Arabic word "migramah," meaning fringe. Arabic weavers back in the 13th century used macramé in 'forming fringes on scarves and veils. Some claim the knot-binding, however, dates back to China during the third century. Sporting knots from this age of lanterns, hangings and ceremonial clothing and some find the standard pan changing knot as an ancient macramé form

While the sources of macramé remain unclear, it is generally assumed that the Moors are responsible for the spread of the craft. The Moors launched macramé into Spain during their voyages from North Africa to Europe, which spread it to France in the 15th century and then to Italy in the 16th century. From there the macramé spread across Europe. Queen Mary II of England had taken a particular interest in the craft earlier in the 17th century. She 'd also asked the ladies to wait. If not by land, then by sea, But the Moors were not merely macramé propagators.

European sailors who tied knots frequently in their daily tasks use this as a way to spend time at sea for the long months. Travelling throughout the world, American and British sailors of the 19th century traded and sold macramé bits they had made during journeys. Crafting knotted items like hammocks and belts, the Macramé was referred to as "square knotting."

Sailors had made macramé objects in hours of the sea and have sold or traded them when they landed, thereby spreading art to places such as China and the New World. British and American mariners of the nineteenth century created macramé hammocks, bell fringes and belts. After the knot, they used most commonly they called the method "square knotting."

In the Victorian era, Macramé was the most famous sailor. Sylvia's favorite Book of Macramé Lace (1882) revealed that "we work on rich trims for black and gold dresses, both for home wear, garden parties, dances, and seaside decorations..." This technique embellished many Victorian homes. Macramé was used to make household items, including clothing, bedding and curtains. Though the craze for macramé waned, in the 1970s, it became more popular as a way to make hangings, clothing items, bedding, small jean shorts, tablecloths, draperies, floor shelves and more. By the early 1980s macramé had once again started to disappear as a decorative trend. Macramé BW But macramé is again becoming famous. This time in jewels, including necklaces, anklets and bracelets. This gem often features handmade glass beads and natural elements, such as gemstones, bone or shell, using mainly square knots.

Macramé may be the millennial DIY of the moment, but it dates back centuries! Macramé has a moment, but that's not the first time. When most people think about macramé, their eyes go back to the bohemian-inspired hills of the 1960s and 1970s. Many say that the knotting started in the 13th century to get to the roots of this practice. Some historians believe the ancient Persians and Babylonians knotted artefacts from the centuries BC. Throughout modern history, macramé was an art form that spread from Arabic countries to the west. Weavers from this part of the world have used different knotting methods to complete tapestries, tapestries and fringed shawls. As these textiles were distributed across Europe, more people started experimenting with knotting. By the 17th century, the practice had reached Britain, where it was introduced in Queen Mary II to the waiting ladies.

Women were not the only macramé people to practice. Seafarers knotted for comfort, but on long journeys, the act of knotting was a means of being occupied and of being bored. Eventually, these sailors continued to spread this practice across Europe. Once they arrived at new ports, they became traders and sold the macramé products they made on the boats. Hammocks, hats and belts were included in popular items.

In the 18th and 19th century the Victorians gradually knotted textiles until sewing machines largely replaced the technique after the industrial revolution. The knotting was popular again in the late sixties and seventies but was quickly out of style in the eighties.

The first stories of macramé are credited to Arab weavers from the 13th century, who used new threads to create knotted decorative threads made of handmade fabrics. China in the third century is also known by the knot pan shift, a set of loops that converge into symbols of infinity to signify immortality. Sailors are also a big part of the history of a profession in the Great Age of Sailing, or around the 1700s to 1830, when they used the knots to wink their blades, bottles and pieces of the ship and their understanding of various types of knots was used to deal creatively!

During the 1970s macramé was used as a standard material, which became tassels, placemat, corner plants, photo frames, hammocks, wall hangings and even bikinis.

While the trend flared away after the 1970s, renewed interest in DIYing videos on YouTube and personal pages for bloggers recently erupted. We're all on the handmade bandwagon.

The apartment dwellers are particularly pleased with the potential of macramé to convert the many hanging-house floors in their entire space to resolve a lack of a yard and to put in more and more buildings and trees (you should also check out this hanging indoor herb garden).

The next time your parents wonder why you're nuts, you might take a bow to the rich history of your craftsmanship centuries ago.

Chapter 2 Benefits of Macramé Pattern

Macramé has proven to be an excellent natural treatment for those undergoing recovery procedures and helps to restore memories once again, making it a unique experience for all. Playing with and tying the ropes, strengthens arms and hands, which helps relax wrist and finger joints. It also helps to calm the mind and soul, as attention is necessary, and the repeated patterns put the weaver in a meditative mood. It is believed that stress is reduced by the fingertips, making macramé knotting a calming task.

Macramé has the added benefit of embracing the self-expression cycle by establishing the underlying purpose concealed within.

As a product of the artistic intervention of scholarly artisans, this human intellectual accomplishment became necessary to incorporate modern architecture requiring the use of other materials for trendy artifacts. While macramé art has been created and used for onward creation in most cultures aimed at achieving both practical and artistic appeal, their end products vary from one culture to the next. These innovations, however, are, by definition, integral parts of cultural growth and are the results of the macramé artisans ' revolutionary accomplishments over the years. The use of adornment knotting distinguishes early cultures and reflected intelligence creation. It is an art that fits all ages and abilities. Today, macramé is experiencing a Revival of the 20th century. Both men and women transition to work with their hands and build not just utilitarian pieces but also decorative ones.

This simplicity and durability, given the importance of macramé, portrays macramé as just a kind of commodity described from a noneconomic viewpoint to its slow production design. Macramé is full of vitality, adaptable, and exploratory and in several respects in product creation and production lends itself for processing and handling. Macramé painting has been a highly valued talent from the earliest times around the world.

Creating pattern that's macramé wishes pattern which are the materials for this type of art work. To make the pattern to create utilizations of cable, the type of for example jute almond or cotton, might choose the types of problems as well as the shades-of the falls. The cable tones should enhance the falls, bracelets and also changes. To keep your materials store them in-boxes plastic situations or organized, after which it, label them accordingly. Macramé bracelet

Health Benefits of Macramé Hangers

Jill Flower Power got it right the first time. There is a health benefit to surrounding your family with green flowers and plants. A great way to grow flowers and plants is to grow them in pots and hang them on macramé.

The macramé plant hangers made great ideas for a craft project or a handmade gift for a friend. The craft is so easy to do; it can be done in just one day or even half a day. Children were taught to macramé by their moms, aunts and grandmas.

In the seventies the art was so favorite that almost every porch would be decorated with macramé hangers in various colors and use different styles in macramé cords. More plant hangers could be found holding indoor plants in the living room and kitchen, where large windows would open towards the backyard, enabling the breeze to enter.

There are new colors of macramé cords now available. Create updated, modern-looking designs that will add color and style to any home as well as provide health benefits for everyone. Remember, making macramé plant hangers for your home or as gifts, and it is not a simple plant hanger. It is a gift of health and happiness for the home. Keeping that in mind, it's time to get your macramé cords and start knotting!

Chapter 3 Terminologies Used in Macramé

While macramé has become quite a popular art, in some patterns there are still many words and abbreviations that people may not be aware of or may not know the meaning of.

Adjacent: next to each other.

Alternating– Attach a knot to one cord and then move to tie another cord to the same knot.

ASK– Alternating knots of the square. This abbreviation is often used in macramé patterns because square knots are commonly used.

Band– A long and smooth piece of macramé.

Bar– A set of knots in the design that create an elevated position.

Bight– A small folded cord portion that is forced through the knot's other sections.

Body– You're working on the main section of the project.

Braid– Braids are sometimes also known as plaits and are formed to loop around each other by connecting three or four cords.

Braided cord– A type of cord consisting of several thinner pieces of cord woven together. Twisted cords tend to be more durable than twisted cords.

Bundles– A series of cords that have been stored.

Knot button– A tight, round decorative knot.

BH– The button's door. Vertical lark head nodes are used to create a loop that could be used for fastening or joining parts.

Chinese Macramé– Knotted designs from China and other countries in Asia.

Combination knot– To create a new type of knot or design feature, use two or more knots.

Cords– Cords is any fiber material that is used to build projects with macramé.

Core– The cord / s running through a project's center and knotting around it. These are sometimes referred to as fillers or main strings.

Crook– The curved part of a cord loop.

Diagonal– A line or row of knots extending from top right to bottom (or vice versa) Diagonal knots such as half-hitch knots are often used in macramé designs.

Diameter– The width usually in millimeters of a cord.

DDH – Half hitch double. This concept of macramé means connecting two knots of half-hitch next to each other.

Fillers– cords that remain at the core of a pattern and are knotted around it. Also referred to as core cords.

Findings– objects and fastenings other than cords that can be used to construct loops, fasteners and other functional objects or decorations in macramé designs. There are examples of ear wires and clasps.

Finishing knot– A knot tied to secure the ends of the cord and to prevent them from unravelling.

Fringe– Cord ends lengths not knotted but left suspended.

Knots of fusion– Another term for knots of combination.

Gusset– A term used to design a 3D project's sides like a bag.

Hitch– A knot commonly used to tie cords to other items.

Interlace– Cords are intertwined and woven together to link various areas.

Cord knotting– the cord used in a design to tie the knots.

LH– Knot of the head of larks.

Loop– The circular or oval shape created by the crossing of two parts of a cord.

Micro-Macramé– Macramé projects made using materials that are delicate or small in diameter. Micro-macramé is often defined as any macramé using cords with a diameter of less than 2 mm.

Mount– An object that is used as part of a macramé project, such as a brace, frame or handle. For example: cords mounted on wooden handles at the beginning of a project with a macramé bag.

Natural– Generally this term is used to refer to cords and refers to any material made from plants, wood and other natural substances such as hemp and cotton.

Netting– A series of knots with open spaces between them. Netting is often used to build things like bags and hangers for plants.

OH– Knot overhand.

Picot– Loops on the sides of a design that stand out. These are seen more often in new trends.

Plait– Cords are plated in an alternating pattern by crossing three or more. Also referred to as a braid.

Scallops– Knots loops created along the edges of the design of a macramé.

Segment– Common knot, cord or design areas.

Seniti– This term, also known as a sonnet, is a single chain of identical knots.

Standing end– The cord end was secured on a macramé board or other surface and did not build knots.

SK– Square knot– A standard knot created by attaching two cords to one or more cords. Stitch– Stitch is sometimes used instead of knot in old patterns.

Synthetic – Man-made fibers such as polypropylene and nylon. Vertical– from top to bottom to top. Vintage– A pattern, knot, or technique popular in or earlier in the early 1900s. Some excellent knots and patterns are still being used unchanged in macramé today, although others have evolved or disappeared.

Weaving– Weaving cords means placing them under each other or over each other.

Working cord– Another term used to knot cord. The cord with which you are currently working.

Chapter 4 Tools And Materials

Macramé Materials

Macramé stylists make use of different types of materials. The materials can be classified in two significant ways; the natural materials and the synthetic materials.

● **Natural Materials**

The qualities of natural materials differ from the synthetic material and knowing these qualities would help you to make better use of them. Natural cord materials existing today include Jute, Hemp, Leather, Cotton, Silk and Flax. There are also yarns made from natural fibers. Natural material fibers are made from plants and animals.

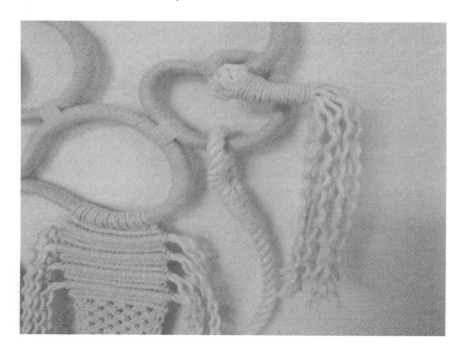

- **Synthetic Materials**

Like natural materials, synthetic materials are also used in macramé projects. The fibers of synthetic materials are made through chemical processes. The major ones are nylon beading cord, olefin, satin cord and parachute cord.

CORD MEASUREMENT

Before you can embark on a macramé project, it is essential that you determine the amount of chord you will need. This includes knowing the length of the required cord and the total number of materials you have to purchase.

Equipment: to measure, you will need a paper for writing, pencil, tape rule and calculator. You would also need some basic knowledge of unit conversion as shared below:

1 inch = 25.4millimeters = 2.54 centimeters

1 foot =12 inches

1 yard = 3 feet = 36 inches

1 yard = 0.9 meters

Note: The circumference of a ring = 3.14 * diameter measured across the ring

Measuring Width

The first thing to do is determine the finished width of the widest area of your project. Once you have this width, pencil it down.

Next, determine the actual size of the materials, by measuring its width from edge to edge.

You can then proceed to determine the type of knot pattern you wish to use with the knowledge of the knot pattern. You must know the width and spacing (if required) of each knots. You should also determine if you want to add more cords to widen an area of if you would be needing extra cords for damps.

With the formula given above, calculate and determine the circumference of the ring of your designs.

Determine the mounting technique to be used. The cord can be mounted to a dowel, ring or other cord. Folded cords affect both the length and width of the cord measurement.

CORD PREPARATION

Though usually rarely emphasized, preparation of the cords and getting them ready for use in Macramé projects is one of the core pillars of the art of Macramé. At times, specialized processes such as conditioning and stiffening of cords need to be carried out before Macramé projects can be begun. In general, however, cord preparation in Macramé is mainly concerned with dealing with cut ends and preventing these ends from unraveling during the course of the project. During the course of a project, constant handing of materials can cause distortion in the ends which can end up having disastrous consequences on your project. Before starting your project, if you do not appropriately prepare particular kinds of cords, like ones that were made by the twisting of individual strands, that cord is likely to come apart, effectively wrecking your project.

Therefore, cord preparation is extremely and incomparably important to the success of any Macramé project, the preparation of each cord is meant to be done during the first step of making any knot, which is the step where you cut out your desired length of cord from the more significant piece.

For cord conditioning, experts recommend rubbing beeswax along the length of the cord. To condition your cord, simply get a bit of beeswax, let it warm up a bit in your hands, and rub it along the cord's length. This will help prevent unwanted tight curls on your cord. Note that beeswax may be applied to both natural and synthetic materials. For synthetic materials however, only Satin and fine Nylon beading cords actually compulsorily require conditioning. After conditioning, inspect your cords for any imperfections and discard useless pieces to ensure the perfection of your project. After conditioning, then comes the actual process of cord preparation. Cords can be prepared (i.e. the ends can be prevented from fraying) through the use of a flame, a knot, tape and glue.

To prevent unraveling of your cord using a flame, firstly test a small piece of the material with the flame from a small lighter. The material needs to melt, not burn. If it burns, then such a cord is not suitable for flame preparation. To prepare using a flame, simply hold the cord to the tip of the flame for 2 to 5 seconds, make sure the cord does not ignite, but melts. Flame preparation is suitable for cords made from olefin, polyester and nylon, and the process is compulsory for the preparation of parachute cords.

Tying knots at the end of the cord is another effective method to prevent fraying. The overhand knot is an all-time favorite, but knots such as the figure 8 knot which is best suited to flexible cords can be used if you think the knot might have to be undone at some point of your project. The Stevedore knot can be used to prevent fraying when using slippery materials.

Glue is another priceless alternative that can be used to prevent fraying at the ends of cords efficiently. However, not all kinds of glue may be used in cord preparation. Only certain brands, such as the Aleen's Stop Fray may be used in cord preparation. Household glue might also be used, but only when diluted with water.

What You Require to Get Started?

You'll need just a few more items to get started after you receive your card. The surface area you will be working on is the most critical supply. I started out with a notebook, mounting my cords on a pencil. My personal favorite is a pillow made of foam which I covered with cloth. Another choice is that of a corkboard piece. This can be purchased at most craft stores. I suggest that it be at least 3/8-inch thick, or finer, and about 11 x 17 inches finer. You need a big enough piece to be able to set it on your lap and lean against a desk with ease.

Make sure you use beautiful sturdy pins to keep your project pined against your work area; I suggest sewing pins or T-pins that they use to hold wigs fixed on the heads of the foam. If your cord is delicate like a satin cord, using the sewing pins with the colored balls on top would be beneficial. We are not going to leave a big hole as often do the T-pins. The only limitations you have are room diameter. Most of the cords are usually about 1 mm thick.

Standard types of macramé supplies include beads, rings, pins, work boards, and beads. Within this main presentation, categories are of many different variations in size, shape and material. Various projects, along with preferences, will be the determining factors in which proper forms of macramé supplies are likely to be used.

Macramé bands come in two basic types: natural and synthetic. Jute is generally a thread-like natural material, while synthetic macramé ropes tend to be like soft ropes. It can be purchased in a variety of colors. The artificial venerable wire is often braided in its composition, rather than twisting.

The rings used for macramé projects vary from crucial chain size or even from small to large hoops. Hoops or loops can also be used as frames so that the vine always joins the nodes attached to it. Copper rings are classical types of macramé supplies, but steel, wood, and plastic are also popular, although they are less used than copper. Rings of different sizes are available for different types of projects, for example, a top hanger or as a bottom point for a bowl.

The shapes of macramé rings aren't just round - a hoop or frame could be square or heart-shaped in addition to the star-, tree-, or animal-shaped (again, despite the different shapes available, the most commonly used body are the round rings).

T pins are a macroscopic supply used to keep work on board. Macramé boards are often rectangular, portable and made of particleboard or cork. T pins penetrate the boards to keep the Macramé project in progress and allow you to work on your project comfortably without any risk of losing your spot or too much movement, which could harm the outcome.

These pins are named around the broad significant cross-section that makes the pins simple to maneuver. Many people doing charity discover that hooked rope strands use a vertical board instead of horizontal surfaces, for example, the table is less dangerous and less tangled for their projects.

Beads are used in many macramé pieces. These come from wood, ceramic and plastic. Folk forms of beads for round, oval, and cylindrical macramé supplies. Wood beads can be light or dark in color. Plastic beads used in the vineyard projects may be transparent or opaque, while the ceramic macramé beads tend to be ornamented, as is the case with painted floral motifs.

- Darcy Gold-Colored Cubed Rings
- Hemptique Hemp cord rollers
- Jute yarns
- Copper-plated Macramé Rings from Pepperell
- Pepper Cotton Macramé Rope

Chapter 5 Basics Of Macramé

There are some direct Macramé basics that you'll need to know to start you off. The surer you are about the system of Macramé, the better time you'll have as you complete one project after another. Figuring out the total cording to use:

You'll need to determine to what degree the length of your cording should be. Yet most endeavors will give you the endorsed estimations, you should have some idea of how this estimation is reached. The pieces of the deals are 3 to several times longer than the piece you mean to make, in any case, since the cording is duplicated down the center for knotting. It is assessed at 7 times longer than the whole amount needed.

For example: if the Macramé project will have an ended length of 1 yard, you'll need to measure your cording at 7 to 8 yards starting with one end then onto the next. By then when each end is increased for knotting it will be two ends, each end being 3 ½ to 4 yards long. Guarantee that you measure the completions liberally since you would incline toward not to miss the mark on cording and need to add to the project. It's much better to have extra cording than it is to run out and remember an unbalanced spot for the procedure.

Making a sampler before you start:

You 're going to have to make a sampler for some Macramé ventures with the aim that you too can see how the string knots are measured and how long. Strong cording can take more time of knotting than durable ones, so that you can test how much cording you need to use to account for this. Create a sampler that measures around 3 inches by 6 inches in order to test the length of the cord in a similar way to see what number of ends the model would require for the distance.

Counting beads and other things:

Beads and other things are regularly added to Macramé's projects to make them captivating, unique and rich in ideas. You can buy beads of all kinds from beading and quality stores, as well as from various wholesalers on the Internet. All you need to do is ensure that the gaps in the beads seem to be large enough for the cord to be strung through with no problem at all. You simply slide the beads on the cord between or in knots to incorporate the beads.

Precisely when you're adding beads to a job, you'll need to scan for beads that are noteworthy and interesting with the objective that they stand out in the Macramé plan. You'll find beads in a collection of styles, sizes, and shapes that consolidates blooms, pictures, and charms. Look for beads that will enhance the Macramé plan that you're working on. You'll need to pick beads with a covering and surface that are going to update your endeavor.

For smaller exercises you'll need to use beads that are sensitive and delicate while your more significant Macramé assignments will need gigantic, ended beads. Take as much time as is needed to hunt for the right beads for your endeavor and set out to try other things with new musings.

Macramé Knot Instructions

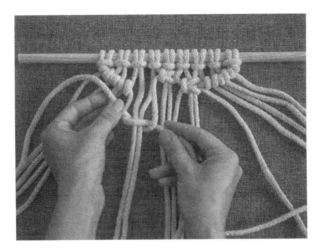

In this part, you will learn the following macramé knots.

- Instructions on how to tie a basic half knot. With special techniques to do it quickly and directly
- Instructions on how to make a secure square knot
- Instructions for making a basic knot over the head
- Instructions to complete the flat macramé pattern design
- Instructions for making macramé spiral design
- Advanced instructions for making a Josephine knot

According to the history of macramé. It is believed that the modern art of the macramé decoration was originated with Arab weavers sometime in the thirteenth century. Arab weavers tied excess threads on the edge of hand-woven fabrics in a decorative knot. Macramé is a very versatile craft. It has been used in the manufacture of many types of jewelery, including necklaces, bracelets, and chokers. It is also used in making everyday objects such as hammocks, hangers and curtains. So, let's tie some macramé knots.

Chapter 6 Types of Basic Macramé Knots

Square Knot

This is an excellent beginning knot for any project and can be used as the foundation for the base of the project. Use lightweight cord for this – it can be purchased at craft stores or online, wherever you get your macramé supplies.

Observe the photos as you move along with this project and take your time to make sure you are using the right string in the right point of the project.

Do not rush, and make sure you have even tension throughout. Practice makes perfect, but with the illustrations to help you, you will find It is not hard at all to create.

Alternating Square Knots

This is the perfect knot to use for basket hangings, decorations, or any projects that are going to require you to put weight on the project. Use a heavier weight cord for this, which you can find at craft stores or online.

Start at the top of the project and work your way toward the bottom. Keep it even as you work your way throughout the piece. Tie the knots at 4-inch intervals, working your way down the entire thing.

Tie each new knot securely before you move on to the one. Remember that the more even you get the better it is.

Work on one side of the piece first, then tie the knot on the other side. you are going to continue to alternate sides, with a knot joining them in the middle, as you can see in the photo.

Again, keep this even as you work throughout.

Bring the knot in toward the center and make sure you have even lengths on both sides of the piece.

Pull this securely up to the center of the cord, then move on to the on the cord.

You are going to gather the cord on one side for the set of knots, then you are going to go back to the other side of the piece to work another set of knots on the other side.

Work this evenly, then you are going to come back to the center.

It is a matter of sequence. Work the one side, then go back to the beginning, then go back to the other side once more. Continue to do this for as long as your cords are, or if you need for the project.

Twofold Half Hitch Knot

Start with at least 3 Lark's head hitches. For this model – we are utilizing 3 Lark's Head hitches. There is an aggregate of 6 strings.

Take the external left line and spot it slantingly over the various 5 ropes. This string is your filler rope. The course and arrangement of this external left rope will decide the example. So simply ensure it's put the manner in which you need over your lines.

Working left to right, make a twofold half hitch tie with the subsequent rope.

Pull your rope tight. Guarantee your external left rope is as yet set askew over the ropes.

Presently make a twofold half hitch tie with the third line.

Presently make a twofold half hitch tie with the fourth line.

Also, prop up until you arrive at the keep going string on the right side. You will see your slanting example of bunches.

Presently, you are going to rehash stages 2-7 yet this time working option to left. So, place the external right rope corner to corner over different ropes.

Instructions to Make a Half Hitch Knot

You can likewise make a flat line of twofold half hitch ties (simply go even rather than askew with that first rope).

There are varieties to the half hitch ties, (similar to significantly increase half hitch hitches), however even with these essential half hitch hitches, you can make incredible examples.

Winding Knot

I think the Spiral bunch is perhaps the prettiest bunch. What's more, luckily – it's one of the most straightforward as well.

You definitely realize how to do the winding bunch.

It's only a recurrent example of half square bunches (first 50% of a square bunch) or half hitch ties. Rather than changing to the right side to finish the square bunch, you simply continue working that left side. The macramé will usually winding. Simply go with it.

To make a thicker rendition of the winding bunch, start with 2 Lark's Head hitches.

To make a single form – start with 1 Lark's Head bunch and make a recurrent example of half hitch ties. Again – your macramé will typically begin to bend. This is the example on the extreme right underneath.

The trickiest piece of this bunch is propping the example up the correct way when it begins to turn.

Macramé has been an excellent method to brighten for a considerable length of time, bringing surface and warmth into a home with hitches that can be assembled in unusual manners to make stand-out tapestries, plant holders, and the sky is the limit from there.

It's anything but difficult to figure out how to macramé because you just need to know a bunch of bunches to make a macramé venture.

Getting Reading to Knot

Before you're prepared to begin figuring out how to macramé, accumulate your provisions and acclimate yourself with some regular macramé terms you'll have to know.

Chinese Crown Knot

Use a pin to help keep everything in place as you are working. Weave the strings in and out of each other as you can see in the photos. It helps to practice with different colors to help you see what is going on. Pull the knot tight, then repeat for the row on the outside. Continue to do this as often as you like to create the knot. You can make it as thick as you like, depending on the project. You can also create more than one length on the same cord.

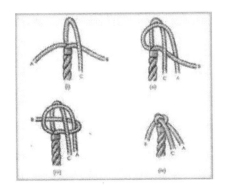

The Barrel Knot

This knot is often used in Macramé projects, most for securing knots at the end as a finish or just to hold the knot from loosening. It is however, also beneficial for firm knots. The Barrel Knot has been in existence for a long time, as evidenced by references made to this handy knot in Macramé literatures.

BASIC DESIGN:

The basic design is the more commonly used Barrel knot and is considered as the standard of Barrel knots. A minimum of fifteen inches length of cord is required to practice this knot.

Fasten the cord to right part of the board. Create a loop by moving the working end anti-clockwise. At the end, allow it to lay vertically.

From below the secure part, roll the working end over the secured part, moving leftward and inward of the loop.

Do this a second time, the new roll on the left of the old. Snug both wraps carefully together without an overlap.

Tighten the knot slowly to make it form and secured, and make sure you avoid any form of twisting or curls in the knot. To achieve the best results, take your time to make cords taut to avoid any slacks in the wraps. You can then tug the secured end slowly to make the loop tight.

The Extended Barrel Knot

As the name implies, the knot is extended by simply adding additional wraps to the knot. You can achieve perfection in the extended barrel knit pattern with constant practice. It is recommended to practice with up to 5 knots, or even more to master this technique.

First of all, repeat the first three steps as described above for basic barrel knot. Add one or two more wrap, each new one always on the left of the previous.

Pull the working cord gently to make the wrapped area tight and then tug at the secured

The Strangle Knot

This variant of the barrel knot is particularly strong and extremely difficult to undo. Thus, it is efficient for use with slippery materials and for points in your project where you need to create a very reliable knot.

First, repeat the first three steps for the basic barrel knot. Be sure to number the segments and commit the number to memory.

Draw the crook (the loop top) closer until it rests between the two cords like a figure eight. Pull both ends gently to make the knot tight while holding the figure eight shape in place.

The Barrel Bead

This is often used to finish a knot horizontally at two ends. It's called the barrel bead because its shape looks like tube beads. It is used in decorative materials where long segment is required to form a fringe.

To create the Barrel Bead knot, you will need a practice with a cord of a minimum length of 30 inches. For the best results, experts recommend a dowel for beginners. However, if a dowel is unavailable, you may also use your fingers, though, your results may not be so spectacular.

PROCEDURE:

In front of the dowel, to the left, put one of the cord's end and secure it for easy handling. Moving right carefully, wrap the cord around the dowel continuously and when you stop, ensure the cord is resting behind the dowel.

Moving rightward from the left, slot the cord's left half beneath the wrapped parts. Move this horizontal crossing down towards the dowel's bottom where it sits on the board.

Moving leftward to the right, do the same for the second half of the cord, allowing the new crossing to rest on the old one.

Pull the knot tight on the dowel and gently remove the dowel but as you do this, keep pushing the knots together.

Do one more to become more experienced. In passing the ends through the new wraps, slot the previous knot in too. Ensure even space between the knot.

The Hanger Knot

The hanger knot has its origin in China. It is a fundamental decorative knot, and is also reliable for the creation of stable loops. To create a link between two overhand knots of opposing direction, the hanger knot is used.

In this instructional manual, two variations of the famous Hanger Knot will be described; one has a top lone loop and possesses a tighter knot. The other is the traditional three loop style that has a rectangular tightened portion at the center. The traditional hanger knot is extremely symbolic to Chinese Buddhism who regard its center structure as good fortune; the triumph of good over evil, good virtues and even regarded as Buddha's heart. A very lovely project that can help you practice the single loop Hanger Knot is the satin dragonfly, in which you will use this knot to make your wings.

TRADITIONAL HANGER KNOT

1.   To begin the THK, repeat the first four steps of the single loop hanger knot technique. For this knot, you need a minimum length of cord of 25 inches. However, do not pull the loops tight. Now you would have three segments;

•   Segment A, which represent the cord part dropping down from the fastened fold.

- Segment B, which represent the part existing the loop from below to drop downward, and;

- Segment C, which point of interception of the two loops, having a semi-loop of its own. The two loops' part at this intersection are known as the crooks.

2. Now, pull the left overhand knot's crook rightward into the crossing of the right overhand knot, such that it slides over segment A and slide below segment B. while doing this, keep the crossing of the right loop straight even as you adjust the size of the knot.

3. Do the same for the right overhand knot cook, this time moving westward till the crook slide beneath segment B and above segment A. You may also increase the size of the knot.

4. Now pull the loops' ends gently to make the knots tight. Once the center is tight, reduce the sizes of the loops.

Chapter 7 Easy Projects For Beginners

Folded Braid Keychain:

This Keychain making is truly simple.

1. Cut three bits of rope somewhat more than twice the length you need for the completed custom keychain.

2. Stack them, even the strands, and wrap one end with a small elastic band a couple of inches from the ends.

3. Do a straightforward mesh. Stop when you are the same distance from the closures as the elastic band is.

4. Circle one end through the keychain. If you'd like, put the elastic band around the two closures to hold them erect.

5. Tie knots in the sections of the bargains to wrap it up.

Macramé Necklace:

Macramé has gotten uncontrollably mainstream over the last few years for its uniqueness, high quality and tasteful look. Making macramé yourself gives you an excellent opportunity to create unique pieces. As of late we shared an instructional exercise for some lovely macramé wall quality structures that you can add to your home or office style. Here we present to you an instructional exercise for a straightforward DIY macramé necklace, ideal for matching with all of your midyear outfits!

Making Your Necklace:

Our DIY macramé necklace uses a progression of the most fundamental macramé knots — the square knot. To make this necklace, you will need a chain and decorative discoveries. We found our copper chain at our nearby jewelry store and afterward used a lobster fastener with two hop rings. We used a copper keyring for our middle, yet don't hesitate to pick another sort of metal that better accommodates your style!

While you're in your jewelry store, you can also choose small beads to fit into your macramé weaving. Just make sure the beads are the same thickness as your string or the beads will fall off! The whiter material is a cotton cord, and the grayish material is a hemp cord. When your materials are ready, follow the step-by-step photographic training exercise below to pleat your DIY macramé necklace.

Heart Keychain

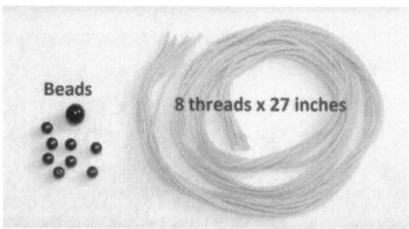

Here to make the keychain you will need 8 smaller beads, one big bead and 8 threads each 27 inches long.

Step 1: You will be making an overhand knot. Take one thread, fold it in half, now form a loop on top of folded thread. This can be done by using your thumb as a guide to how long the loop should be. Then hold the thread at this length so that the loop is isolated.

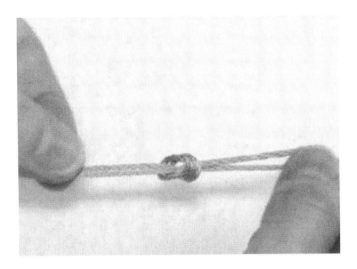

Step 2: while keeping the loop isolated, create another loop with the rest of the thread and then place the original loop through the new loop while keeping hold of the original loop and then when through you can pull to tighten. You should end up with something like the picture below.

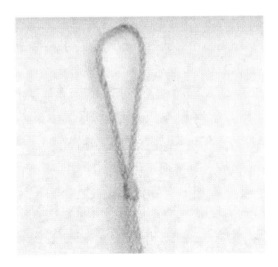

This is what your overhand knot should look like.

Step 3: Take another one of your threads, place it over your previous thread with the knot in it ensuring that the knot is in the middle of the new thread you have just chosen.

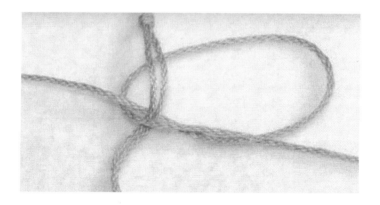

Step 4: Now you are going to tie a square knot. Take the left-hand side of the thread that you have just lay down (the one without the knot) and place it over the thread above it and under the thread on the right. Then take the right-side thread and thread it under the thread at the bottom and under the left-hand side and through the loop that has been created by the left-hand thread. Simultaneously, pull the threads on the left and right side so that it tightens, and a knot is created.

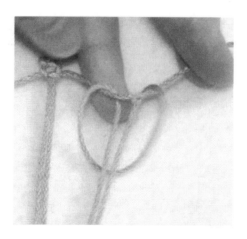

Step 5: Take the single thread on the right, place over the two threads in the middle and under the left thread. Now take the left thread under the two threads in the middle and under the loop created on the right. Pull to tighten (both sides at the same time) and create your knot.

Step 6: Take the single thread on the left, then take the single thread on the right. Ensure that both threads are horizontal. For now, you will only be working with the right so you can set the left side down until later.

Step 7: Take a new single thread, fold it in half, make sure there is a loop created at the top. Then place the thread behind the single thread on the right and fold over the top. Now, pull the two loose threads through the middle of the loop so that it looks as above. Then pull the threads so that the thread tightens, and you will end up with a Lark's head knot.

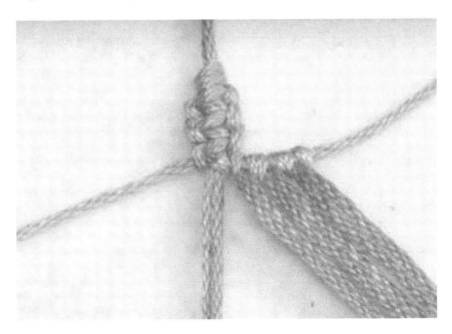

Take two more single threads and repeat step 7 until you end up with two more Lark's head knots on the right.

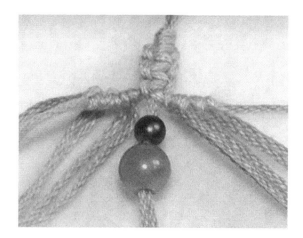

Step 8: Take the left single thread, which should be horizontal as stated earlier. Then create three more Lark's head knots on the left single thread. It should look like the picture above.

Step 9: Now you should have three Lark's head knots on each side.

Step 10: You should now have two threads in the middle. Take a small bead and thread it onto the two threads.

Step 11: Take a big bead and place on the same thread pushing it to the top so that your macramé piece looks like the one in the picture.

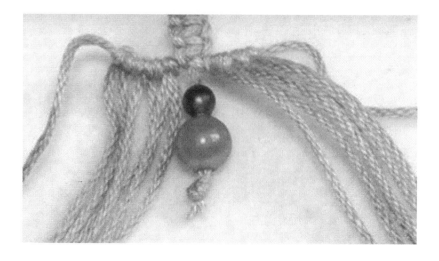

Step 12: Tie a simple over hand knot at the end of the middle thread, under the beads, so that the beads are locked in place. There are instructions above on how to do this.

Step 13: Take a pair of scissors and cut the loose thread at the end of the knot leaving just the knot.

Refer to the image above.

Step 14: From your left group of threads, take the first on the right and place it horizontally across the other threads in the bunch. Then take the thread next to it, loop it over the horizontal thread, under itself, then using the same thread loop it over the horizontal thread again and finally through the loop created. Pull to secure the knot tightly. You will have a half hitch knot.

Step 15: Repeat this step with each thread until you all threads on the left have been done.

Step 16: Take the next thread, directly under the half hitch knot, on the right. Pull this thread across horizontally and repeat the process of creating the half hitch knot.

Step 17: Repeat this process 6 more times so you have 8 half hitch knots in total like the picture below. (excluding the one at the bottom)

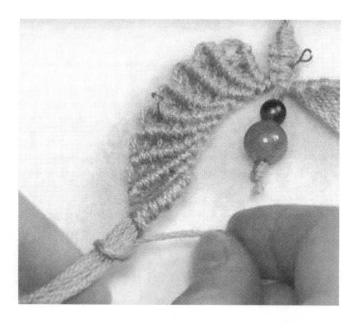

Step 18: Here you will be creating the knot at the bottom of the left side.

Step 19: Take the first thread on the right of the bottom knot. Then take the thread next to it, loop it over the horizontal thread, under itself, then using the same thread loop it over the horizontal thread again and finally through the loop created. Pull to secure the knot tightly. You will have a half hitch knot.

Step 20: Take the thread used to create the half hitch knot and place around both horizontal threads, under itself, then using the same threads loop them over the horizontal threads and finally through the loop created. Pull to tighten

Step 21: Then take the thread just used for the horizontal thread and place across the remaining threads. You should have three horizontal threads. Take the threads next to it and wrap it around the three horizontal threads to create a half hitch knot. Take the next thread and wrap it around both horizontal threads, under itself, then using the same threads loop them over the horizontal threads and finally through the loop created. Pull to tighten

Step 22: Repeat this process, add one thread each time, until you get to the last thread. Your macramé piece should look like the image above.

This is what your finished left side should look like. If you have made any mistakes it is okay to go back and change them. The last half hitch knot can be hard to follow but use the pictures to aid you and you will succeed.

For the completion of the right side, start in the same way you did for the left side. This is the same process and if you completed the left side you shouldn't find it too hard. Repeat the steps given previously.

When completed it should look like the illustration given above. Don't worry if you don't get it first time. You can always undo your stitching and try again.

Step 23: With the hanging threads from both the left and right side, pull to make sure they are vertical. The threads should be together as one group.

Step 24: Cut a piece of the thread, around 4 inches and fold it in half to use. Now place this piece of thread in the middle of the bunch but sitting on top and the two ends facing the top as in the picture (purple thread).

Step 25: Take a single thread from the group of threads. Wrap it around the group of threads as shown above.

Step 26: Continue to wrap the thread around the group of threads until there is only a short portion of the single thread left. There should have been a loop created by the short piece of thread cut earlier (purple thread

in photo). Place the end of the thread (purple) through the loop as shown, pull the two ends of the loose thread (purple) at the top so that the loose thread (purple) will come out completely. The end of the single thread becomes trapped inside the loop creating a knot.

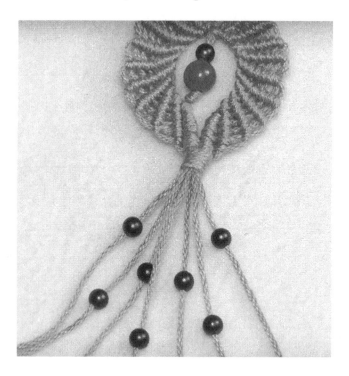

Step 27: You should have several threads hanging loose from the knot just created. Place a small bead through each thread and show them to have the same intervals between them. They should be staggered creating the pattern shown.

Step 28: Now do an overhand knot at the end of each bead to secure it in place. Refer to earlier instructions on how to complete this.

Step 29: Trim the remaining threads from underneath the knots.

This is what your final macramé piece should look like. You will have a beautiful keychain to use yourself or gift to someone.

Chapter 8 Easy Projects for Beginners II

Serenity Bracelet

(Note: if you are familiar with the flat knot, you can move right along into the next pattern)

This novice bracelet offers plenty of practice using one of micro macramé's most used knots. You will also gain experience beading and equalizing tension. This bracelet features a button closure and the finished length is 7 inches.

Knots Used:

Flat Knot (aka square knot)

Overhand knot

Supplies:

White C-Lon cord, 6 ½ ft., x 3

18 - Frosted Purple size 6 beads

36 - Purple seed beads, size 11

1 - 1 cm Purple and white focal bead

26 - Dark Purple size 6 beads

1 - 5 mm Purple button closure bead

(Note: the button bead needs to be able to fit onto all 6 cords)

Instructions:

Take all 3 cords and fold them in half. Find the center and place on your work surface as shown:

Now hold the cords and tie an overhand knot, loosely, at the center point. It should look like this:

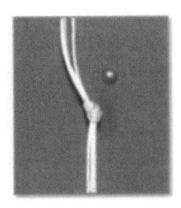

1. We will now make a buttonhole closure. Just below the knot, take each outer cord and tie a flat knot (aka square knot). Continue tying flat knots until you have about 2 ½ cm.

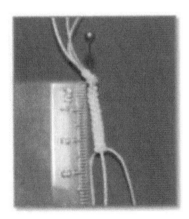

2. Undo your overhand knot and place the ends together in a horseshoe shape.

3. We now have all 6 cords together. Think of the cords as numbered 1 through 6 from left to right. Cords 2-5 will stay in the middle as filler cords. Find cord 1 and 6 and use these to tie flat knots around the filler cords. (Note: now you can pass your button bead through the opening to ensure a good fit. Add or subtract flat knots as needed to create a snug fit. This size should be fine for a 5mm bead). Continue to tie flat knots until you have 4 cm worth. (To increase bracelet length, add more flat knots here and the equal amount in step 10).

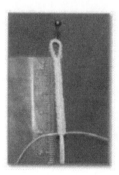

4. Separate cords 1-4-1. Find the center 2 cords. Thread a size 6 frosted purple bead onto them, then tie a flat knot with cords 2 and 5.

5. We will now work with cords 1 and 6. With cord 1, thread on a seed bead, a dark purple size 6 beads and another seed bead. Repeat with cord 6, and then separate the cords into 3-3. Tie a flat knot with the left 3 cords. Tie a flat knot with the right 3 cords.

6. Repeat step 4 and 5 three times.

7. Find the center 2 cords, hold together and thread on the 1cm focal bead. Take the next cords out (2 and 5) and bead as follows: 2 size 6 dark

purple beads, a frosted purple bead, and 2 dark purple beads. Find cords 1 and 6 and bead as follows: 2 frosted purple beads, a seed bead, a dark purple bead, a seed bead, 2 frosted purple beads.

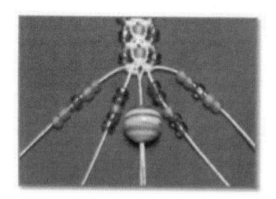

8. With cords 2 and 5, tie a flat knot around the center 2 cords. Place the center 4 cords together and tie a flat knot around them with outer cords 1 and 6.

9. Repeat steps 4 and 5 four times.

10. Repeat step 3.

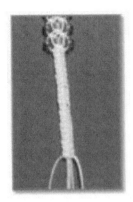

11. Place your button bead on all 6 cords and tie an overhand knot tight against the bead. Glue well and trim the cords.

Lantern Bracelet

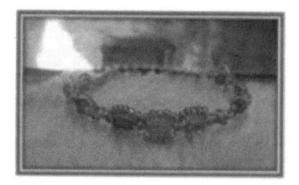

This pattern may look simply, but please don't try it if you are in a hurry. This one takes patience. Don't worry about getting your picot knots all the same shape. Have fun with it! The finished bracelet is 7 ¼ inches in length. If desired, add a picot knot and a spiral knot on each side of the center piece to lengthen it. This pattern has a jump ring closure.

Knots Used:

Lark's Head Knot

Spiral Knot

Picot Knot

Overhand Knot

Supplies:

3 strands of C-Lon cord (2 light brown and 1 medium brown) 63-inch lengths

Fasteners (1 jump ring, 1 spring ring or lobster clasp)

Glue - Beacon 527 multi-use

8 small beads (about 4mm) amber to gold colors

30 gold seed beads

3 beads (about 6 mm) amber color (mine are rectangular, but round or oval will work wonderfully also)

Note: Bead size can vary slightly. Just be sure all beads you choose will slide onto 2 cords (except seed beads).

Instructions:

1. Find the center of your cord and attach it to the jump ring with a lark's head knot. Repeat with the 2 remaining strands. If you want the 2-tone effect, be sure your second color is NOT placed in the center, or it will only be a filler cord and you will end up with a 1 tone bracelet.

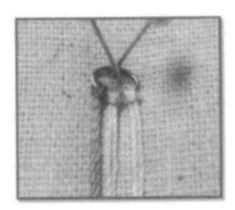

2. You now have 6 cords to work with. Think of them as numbered 1 thorough 6, from left to right. Move cords 1 and 6 apart from the rest. You will use these to work the spiral knot. All others are filler cords. Take cord

number 1 tie a spiral knot. Always begin with the left cord. Tie 7 more spirals.

3. Place a 4mm bead on the center 2 cords. Leave cords 1 and 6 alone for now and work 1 flat knot using cords 2 and 5.

4. Now put cords 2 and 5 together with the center strands. Use 1 and 6 to tie a picot flat knot. If you don't like the look of your picot knot, loosen it up and try again. Gently tug the cords into place then lock in tightly with the next spiral knot.

Notice here how I am holding the picot knot with my thumbs while pulling the cords tight with my fingers. If you look closely you may be able to see that I have a cord in each hand.

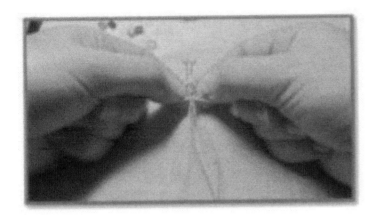

5. Tie 8 spiral knots (using left cord throughout pattern).

6. Place a 4mm bead on the center 2 cords. Leave cords 1 and 6 alone for now and work 1 flat knot using cords 2 and 5. Now put cords 2 and 5 together with the center strands. Use strands 1 and 6 to tie a picot flat knot.

7. Repeat steps 5 and 6 until you have 5 sets of spirals.

8. Next place 5 seed beads on cords 1 and 6. Put cords 3 and 4 together and string on a 6 mm bead. Tie one flat knot with the outermost cords.

Repeat this step two more times.

Now repeat steps 5 and 6 until you have 5 sets of spirals from the center point, thread on your clasp. Tie an overhand knot with each cord and glue well. Let dry completely. As this is the weakest point in the design, I advise trimming the excess cords and gluing again. Let dry.

Chapter 9 Decorative Macramé Patterns for your Home and Garden

Macrame Plant Holder

This is not the macramé of your grandma. All right, maybe it is, but at some point, something makes a comeback or another right? I love this macramé plant holder's smooth and textured feel. And the best part, the best part? It can be done in a few minutes! I'm all about basic projects that can be completed in a couple of minutes.

Macramé plant holder

This is a perfect project to make extra yarn scraps for friends and family. You can use live plants in your bowl, or you can use a fake one if you're a plant killer like me. Any watering? No watering? That's up my alley — let's start now!

Macramé Plant Holder Materials

- Metal or wooden ring
- Yarn
- Potted plant

Methods

1. Cut four different yarn lengths. Mine were about 2 feet long–you want to make sure that your plant holder is enough to finish! You may need to make the yarn strands even longer, depending on how big your planter is.

2. Fold half the strands of your yarn, then loop the folded end of your chain. Take the loose ends and pull them through the yarn loop you created.

3. Split the yarn into four yarn groupings of two yarn strands each.

4. Measure several centimeters (I just looked at it) and tie each of the groupings together. Ensure that the knots are about the same length.

5. Document this ad Take the left path of each group and add it to the right way of the next grouping. Keep the knots a little deeper, from the first set of knots only an inch or two. I know it sounds complicated, but it's not, I swear! Take the two external threads and bind them together to create a circular network.

6. Tie one additional round of knots, repeating the process of knotting each group's left strand to the right strand of the next.

Bring the ties pretty close to the last round you made—just half or two inches away this time.

7. Tie all the threads of yarn a little under the last round of knots you made around one inch. Cut off the extra yarn to create a beautiful tassel.

Amazing Macramé Curtain

Macramé Curtains give your house the feel of that beach house look. You don't even have to add any trinkets or shells—but you can, if you want to. Anyway, here's a great Macramé Curtain that you can make!

What you need:

Laundry rope (or any kind of rope/cord you want)

Curtain rod

Scissors

Pins

Lighter

Tape

Instructions:

Tie four strands together and secure the top knots with pins so they could hold the structure down.

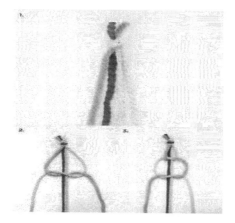

Take the strand on the outer right part and let it cross over to the left side employing passing it through the middle. Tightly pull the strings together and reverse what you have done earlier.

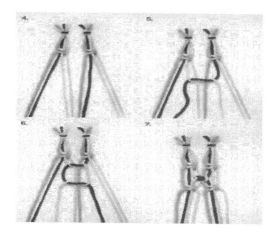

Repeat crossing the thread over four more times for the thread you now have in front of you. Take the strand on the outer left and let it pass through the middle, and then take the right and let it cross over the left side. Repeat as needed, then divide the group of strands to the left, and also to the right. Repeat until you reach the number of rows you want.

You can now apply this to the ropes. Gather the number or ropes you want—10 to 14 is okay, or whatever fits the rod, with good spacing. Start knotting at the top of the curtain until you reach your desired length. You can burn or tape the ends to prevent them from unraveling.

Braid the ropes together to give them that dreamy, beachside effect, just like what you see below.

That's it, you can now use your new curtain!

Macramé Charm and Feather Décor

Charms and feathers always look cool. They just add a lot of that enchanting feeling to your house, and knowing that you could make Macramé décor with charms and feathers take your crafting game to new heights! Check out the instructions below and try it out for yourself!

What you need:

Stick/dowel

feathers and charms with holes (for you to insert the thread in)

Embroidery/laundry rope (or any other rope or thread that you want)

Instructions:

Cut as many pieces of rope as you want. Around 10 to 12 pieces is good, and then fold each in half. Make sure to create a loop at each end, like the ones you see below:

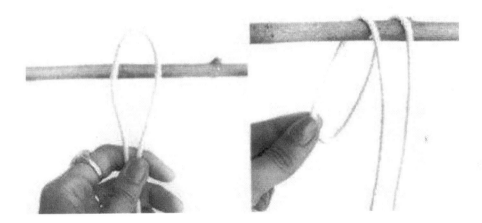

Then, go and loop each piece of thread on the stick.

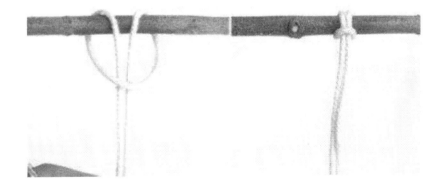

Make use of the square knot and make sure you have four strands for each knot. Let the leftmost strand cross the next two strands and then put it over the strands that you have in the middle. Tuck it under the middle two, as well.

Check under the strands and let the rightmost strand be tucked under the loop next to the left-hand strand.

Tighten the loop by pulling the outer strands together and start with the left to repeat the process on the next four strands. You will then see that a square knot has formed after tightening the loops together.

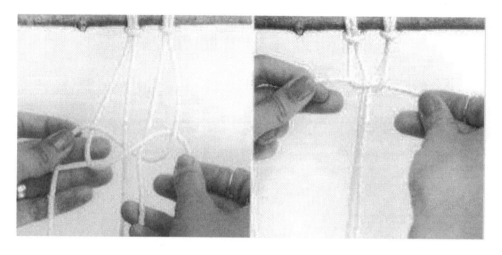

Connect the strands by doing square knots with the remaining four pieces of rope and then repeat the process again from the left side. Tighten the loop by pulling the outer strands together and start with the left to repeat the process on the next four strands. You will then see that a square knot has formed after loops have been tightened together.

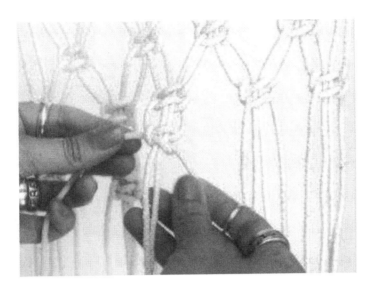

You can then do a figure-eight knot and then just attach charms and feathers to the end. Glue them in and burn the ends for better effect!

Plant Hanger Bella

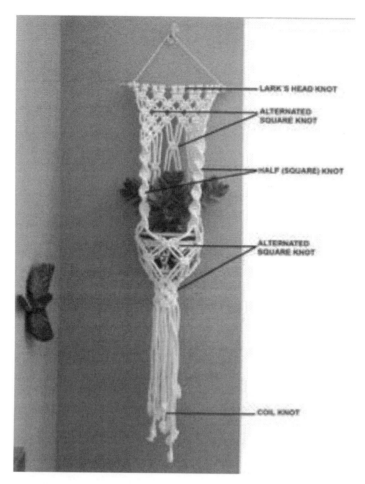

Description: Plant hanger of 60 cm (not counting the fringe)

Supplies: 6 strands of the cord of 13 feet and 1,5 inches (4 meters), 4 strands of 16 feet and 4,8 inches (5 meter) and a wooden stick of 11,8 inches (30cm)

Used Knots: A half knot, Lark's Head knot, (Alternating) square knot and Coil knot

Directions (step-by-step):

1. Fold all strands in half and tie them to the wooden stick with Lark's Head knot. The longest strands are on the outer side (2 strands at the left side and 2 at the right).

2. Make 4 rows of alternating square knots. (See knot guide for explanation)

3. In the 5th row you only make 2 alternating square knots on the right and 2 on the left.

4. In the 6th row you only tie 1 alternating square on each side.

5. Then, with the 4 strands on the side, you tie 25 half (square) knots. Do this for both sides, left and right side.

6. Take 4 strands from the middle of the plant hanger, first drop down 2,4 inches (6 cm of no knots) and then tie a square knot with the 4 center strands. Now with the 4 strands next to the middle, Drop down 3,15 inches (8 cm of no knots), and tie a square knot. Do this for both sides (left and right).

7. Drop down 2,4 inches (6 cm of no knots) and tie 2 (alternated) square knots by taking 2 strands from both sides (right and left group). Then 3 alternating square knots with the other groups. These knots must be about at the same height where the strands with the half knots have ended.

8. Take the 2 outer strands of the left group, which you made 25 half knots, and take the 2 outer strands of the group on the right. First dropping down 2,4 inches (6 cm of no knots), you tie a square knot with these 4 strands.

9. Do the same with the rest of the strands left over, make groups of 4 strands and tie alternated square knots on the same height as the one you made in step 8. Drop down 2,4 inches (6 cm of no knots) and make another row of alternated square knots using all strands.

10.   Drop down 2,4 inches (6 cm of no knots) and make 5 rows of alternated square knots. Be careful: this time leave NO space in between the alternated square knots and you make them as tight as possible.

11.   Drop down as many inches/cm as you want to make the fringe and tie at all ends a coil knot.

12.   Then cutoff all strands, directly under each coil knot.

Chapter 10 Tips and Tricks on Macramé

If you are an amateur or learner to the specialty of macramé, here are some fundamental tips to assist you with keeping away from botches and be fully operational in your new interest. Hitching is the way to macramé, yet before you get moving, here are a few hints that will spare you time and dissatisfaction when you are simply beginning to learn.

Become familiar with the essential bunches with hemp line, as it is anything but difficult to work with and simple to fix ties.

When you have the fundamental macramé ties down, use nylon cording for your underlying gems ventures, as opposed to silk. It's a lot simpler to evacuate tying botches.

Searing the closures just works with nylon cording.

Make a straightforward undertaking board to use as your work territory. It's anything but difficult to make, and can go anyplace, making your undertaking truly versatile.

Continuously twofold watch that the string you intend to utilize fits through the dot openings (before you start!)

To shield the finishes from fraying, tie a bunch toward the finish of the rope. You can utilize clear nail clean on the parts of the bargains to shield them from fraying too, and this additionally stiffens the closures, making it simpler to string those small seed globules. You can likewise utilize a "no quarrel" fluid found in texture stores to do a similar activity.

Spare extra bits of cording to rehearse new bunches with. The way into a cleaned search for your piece is uniform tying. Careful discipline brings about promising results!

If you don't have any t nails to hand, use corsage pins to make sure about your work. If utilizing calfskin cording, make an x with two pins to make sure about the line set up so as not to cut the rope. Spot the pins on either side of the line crossing in an askew way, similar to a X to make sure about the string set up.

Remember that each of these knots is going to be the foundation of the other projects that you create, so you are going to have to take the time to get familiar with each of them – and practice them until they are what you need them to be. You aren't likely going to get them perfectly right away – so take the time to make sure you do it right before you move on to the one.

Don't worry if you don't get it at first, it's going to come with time, and the more time you put into it, the better you are going to become. It does take time and effort to get it right, but the more time and effort you put into it, the better you are going to be.

But you look at the price, and you suddenly put it down. You would love to be able to support the artist, and you would love to fill your house with all kinds of handmade and unique items, but when it comes down to it, you simply can't afford to pay those kinds of prices. Of course, it is all worth it, but when you can't afford it, you can't afford it.

Yet, you don't walk away empty handed. You now have more inspiration than you know what to do with. You want to make and create. You want to do something that is going to catch the eye of your friends and family, and you want to turn it into something that is amazing. When it comes to the world of hand-crafted items, you are going to find that there really is no end to the ways you can show off your creativity by the things that you make.

But you have creativity, but you don't know what to do with it. You want to make something, but when it comes to the actual execution of the craft, you feel lost.

And that's where this comes in. In it, you are going to find all kinds of new knots that you can then use to create whatever it is you want to create. You are going to find that there is no end to the ways that you can use your skills to create whatever it is you wish.

It can be difficult at first, but the more you put into it, the easier it's all going to become until it is just second nature to you. I know you are going to fall in love with each and every aspect of this hobby, and when you know how to work the knots, you are going to want to make them in all the ways you possibly can.

Don't worry about the colors, and don't worry if you don't get it right the first time. This is going to give you everything you need to make it happen the way you want it to, and it is going to show you that you really can have it all with your macramé projects.

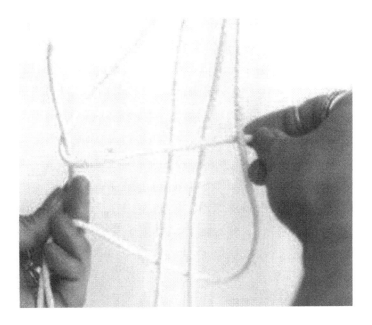

Using decent quality rope

A wide range of macramé-fitting cotton, acrylic, nylon, and twine cords with a rope-like twist are available in art and home stores. Personally, I consider using a cotton rope at least 3 mm in diameter. Cotton clothes come in two kinds. Twisted and twisted cotton bandage. The braided cotton rope is woven into one continuous rope by six (or more) threads. 3-Strand rope (sometimes called a 3-ply) where the fibers are twisted. I saw it in four strands but it seems like a typical 3-strand thread. I love it because working with it is really easy, incredibly strong and robust, and it unravels to make a very good fringe at the ends.

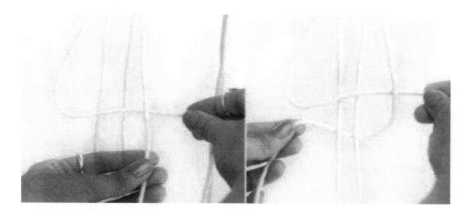

Keep it simple

There are so many different knots to use in macramé. A strong first-node is a basic node to know in square. There are two ways of creating the node: a rectangular node, and alternates a rectangular node. The whole foundation of most the macramé out there these days is this knot, and a wonderfully easy knot for beginners to try.

Keep your tension even

This one has to be practice. The strength with which the knots are tightened affects the consistency of their size. Practice over and over until you find a rhythm and see your knots are consistent. You 're going to need to find a balance between knotting to lose and having your work look shoddy and knotting too tight.

Get involved and have fun

The easiest way to do something is to get the proper help. The same holds true for macramé-learning. Join a fellow member of the amateur macramé. You will find answers to your questions, will be inspired and will share information. Expressing your imagination by macramé is one of the best parts of the voyage. Let your imagination go wild, and construct something from the heart.

Attend A Workshop

Teaching yourself is fun, but we suggest you attend a workshop if you have any in your area. You get to get in touch with so many like-minded people, and even leave with not only your very own finished work of art, but also new friends! We're going on a full US workshop tour this summer, where we're going to teach wall hanging, plant hangers, mobile phones, chandeliers, headpieces and more! Check out our tour page for a city near you.

Save Your Left-Over Cord

You should make some attempts while you are training, and try again. And having the right length of JUST cord can be your biggest obstacle. You don't want a little string, because it can be hard to add extra to your piece. We also recommend that you make at least 10 percent more mistakes than you think you should, just to be safe.

In the new Modern Macramé book, we have a detailed step-by-step variable on how to evaluate how often rope you need for your macramé.

That's in mind, you could end up with an extra cord at the end of your project! Not to worry about that! We recommend that you save all of your remaining strings. You can add the used cord to future projects, and if you stay tuned, we'll be launching a very special FREE pattern in the next few weeks, which is a fun way to reuse your scraps.

Chapter 11 Advanced Macramé Techniques

M any Macramé tasks are easy to finish. Each job has a great deal of models to create it your own. At any time, you feel used to knotting, you are inclined to be in a position to produce your routines and make some genuinely exceptional cloths. Consider ways you can change a number of these Subsequent Macramé ideas:

- Wall-hangings

- Planters

- Crucial chains

- Hanging chairs

- Belts

- Antiques

Fringe on special fabrics

Millennials might have attracted Macramé past, but individuals of ages can indeed love and fall in love for this particular craft.

Button square knots: begin out with three square knots Then keep onto screw pliers by the back amid the horn cables before their original. Publish a rectangle under the bottom of this button to finish.

Cosmetic Dentistry: used making jewelry or to get Special knots such as Celtic and Chinese. These two approaches go perfectly with handmade jewelry and precious stones, for example semi-precious stones, crystals, or pearls. These Macramé knots usually are intricate and could possibly have a while to know.

Double-hitch knot: that Macramé knot is created by Generating two half hitch knots you afterward a second. Yank on the knots attentively.

Half Hitch knot: place Inch cable through your job Area (pin therefore that the cable will not proceed). At the finish of the cable that's been hauled across the unmoving cable is drawn under the cable and pulled the loop which has been shaped.

Half knot: One of the normal Macramé knots to create. A fifty% knot is really an ordinary knot, you start with four strings. Put it using this loop produced by the center cable together with your hand cable. Tug to Fasten the knot.

Overhand knot: Just One of the Most Often used knots in Macramé. Start out with developing a loop by way of one's own cable. Pull the knot carefully.

Square knots: construct out of this fifty-five percent knot to Produce the square knot. Take your righthand cable behind the center strings and then send it about the left-handed cable. Only choose the left-handed cable and place it throughout the ideal hand by simply moving the middle strings and pull.

Ever wanted to be able to make your own bracelets & designer handbag, but did not comprehend just how or did not have the appropriate resources? You have probably experienced such a difficulty. Well, macramé design is exactly what the physician ordered.

Macramé is just a sort of fabric which works by using knotting. Materials that are utilized from the macramé process comprise jute, linen, strings got out of cotton twine, yarn, and hemp. It's a procedure for knotting ropes codes or strings collectively with one another to check something. This item might be described as a necklace jewelry, necklace, etc. Macramé designs can possibly be made complicated if different knots have been united to produce one layout or complicated.

Chapter 12 Advanced Macramé Pattern

Designer Hat

This Macramé Hat has a round top and a beautifully decorated brim with tiny triangles. It can also be used as a Macramé basket. For this, it is recommended to use a material which is not extremely flexible, or it doesn't keep its shape. Bonnie Braid is used in the illustration given below.

A medium-sized hat with dimensions of 28 inches around with a 1.5-inch brim will be created here. If you want to make a smaller or larger hat, I have provided you with cord measurements.

It is a simple project for beginners. Be sure to practice the decorative knots stated under before you attempt to make this personalized hat if you're new to Macramé.

Materials Required:

• 4mm Cord Material (114 yards)

• Fabric Glue

• Tape Measure

• Pins and Project Board

Knots used:

• Alternating Square Knots (ASK)

- Larks Head Knot

- Overhand Knot

- Double Half Hitch (DHH)

Step by Step Instructions:

1. For the hat created here, you will need to cut 56 cords, which should be 2 yards in length each. For a 24-inch hat cut one holding cord 36 inches long and 48 other strings, each of which must be 2 yards in length. For a 32-inch hat, you will need a total of 64 cords, 2.5 yards each. For a hat above or below these sizes, increase or decrease the size as needed (2 strings per inch). The number of cords you use should be multiples of 4. Fix the split ends of the cord with a tape. It would prevent the unraveling of the strings. Tie the holding string with your work station horizontally, and make sure it is stretched firmly. Fold in half one of the two-yard strings, and place it under the holding string, so that it lies near the center.

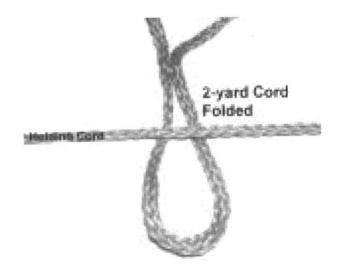

2. Place the ends over the holding cord to complete the formed Larks Head knot, going downward. Move them underneath the folded line. Stiffly close.

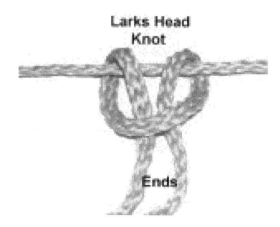

3. Attach each end of Half Hitch knot by leading the rope over and below the holding string. It will ride over the thread you're working with when you set it down.

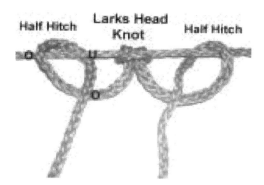

4. Repeat the steps from step 1 to 3, by wrapping the remaining strings to your holding string. Start working from the center and move to the ends. There must be an equivalent amount of strings in both directions.

5. For creating the edge for your Macramé Hat, chose any eight cords and marked them from cord 1 to 8 from left towards right. All the triangle designs are created using eight strings, so split them out now, before you start working on the triangles. Make a Square Knot with 2-4 strings. You only have one filler the string 3. Tightly firm it, so it sets against your mounted knots. Do it again with the strings 5, 6, and 7. This time the filler is cord 6.

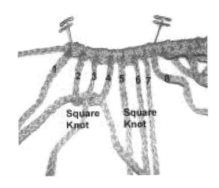

6. Now attach the other Square Knot under the first two, using strings 3 - 6 (two fillers

-- 4 and 5). Tighten the knots firmly, so it rests over the knots above it.

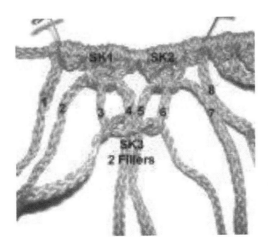

7. Move the cord number 1 with the left side of the three knots that forms a triangular shape. Lock it, so that it's tight since it is a holding string. Join the cords 2, 3, and 4 to it through the Double Half Hitches.

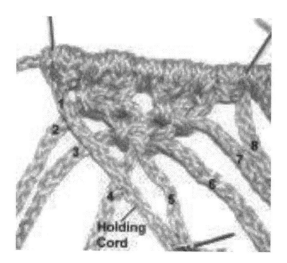

8. Move the string 8 along the right edge of the triangle, and fix it as well. Attach strings 5, 6, and 7 with it with a Double Half Hitch knot. Make sure not to attach the holding cord 1 with it, or the design will be unbalanced.

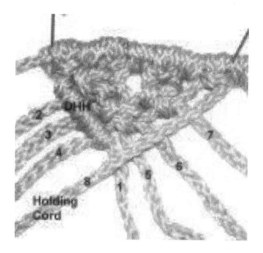

9. Make a cross using the firming string 1 and 8, and extent all the strings in a manner so it will be easier for you to see them. Attach a Square Knot

using cords 1, 4, 5, and 8. Use cords 8 and 1 as the fillers. Firmly tie the knots, so that the knot stays below triangle level.

10. Repeat steps 5 to 9, to make additional triangle with the help of your next eight cords. Attach a Square Knot from the first line, with cords 6 and 7, and 2 and 3 from the second side. Tighten it so under each triangle it meets up with the Square Knot.

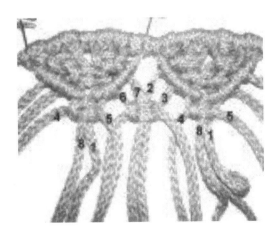

11. Repeat step from step no 5 to 10 with the help of remaining clusters of cords. When you reach the final triangle figure for your Macramé Hat, connect this triangle to the first triangle you created, to make a complete circle. Now begin turning upside down the brim of your Macramé Cap.

Although actually the right side of the triangles is on the opposite side of the hat. Keep in mind that the brim which is created will be folded in a manner, so the orders are swapped. It can be also be seen in the picture attached below, which is showing the rear side of the triangles at the moment, where you will be doing your work. Attach a Square Knot with the help of strings 2 and 3 from the first triangle that you created, with 6 and 7 from the last triangle. It is just what you have done in the previous step, and the only difference is that the cords come from each edge of the brim

Identify the edges of your holding string used in the tying process. Once you identify your holding cord, tie an Overhand knot and glue it, and tie another one on the upper side of the first knot. Trim the excess by 2 inches, fold them under the mounting knots, and apply a generous amount of glue so it holds the knots in its place. Don't forget that the triangles should be at the back side and not on the front.

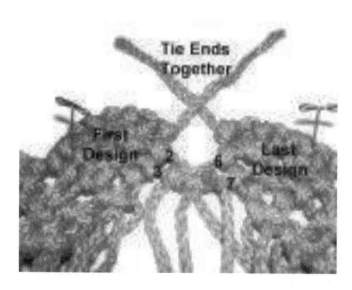

12. To create the top part, you will link a row of Alternating Square knots (ASK) using 4 cords per knot, two working cords, and two fillers. Starting

at the place where the two ends were connected in phase 7 is easiest, then continuing around the entire route. To create the next row, alternate the strings. Keep the brim on the inner side while creating your hat. Mentally number each set with four cords. Strings No.1 and No.4 act as the working cords, while two and three are the filler cords. Combine 3 and 4 with 1 and 2 from next knot over to alternate for next lines. And the current knot lies between the two above.

13. Stop tying Alternating Square Knot when your Macramé hat is at least 7 inches in height which starts from the lower end of the brim, till the row of knots that you are currently working on. Keep in mind you'll cover the bottom, so you'll only have a couple more rows to add to the top.

14. Choose 12 cords that are coming from the three Alternating Square Knots. Visually mark each set with four cords as A, B, and C. Push all the four strings from the set B to the inside of the Macramé hat.

15. Use the cords 3 and 4 from set A (that is at the extreme left side), with strings No.1 and No.2 from your set C (that is at the extreme right side).

With these four ropes, tie securely a Square Knot over the gap left by the strings you just put through. Tighten the knots firmly. So, the top edge of your hat will appear more rounded.

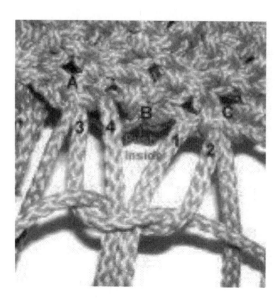

16. Repeat the previous step by dropping all the remaining knots by pushing the knots inside. This will fasten the top of the Macramé Hat. Do steps 3 and 4 two more times, until you've been all the way back. Move the remaining cords into the inside until you are done.

17. Take the right side of the hat up. Note, that the front of the triangles at the top is the bottom, and while you're focusing on these final stages, they can be seen around the lower lip. Tie two very tight overhead knot using two cords at a time but from two different knots. If there are some wide gaps, begin crossing the void by choosing cords from each side of it. Hook one knot, apply adhesive to the thread, then tie the knot next to the previous. Trim the excess cords after you tie the knots. As the strings are taped at the ends, you can simply cut them off to identify which cords are used. After you are done with tying all the knots, let the glue dry and cut off any extra material. Switch the Designer Hat's brim outwards, arrange it at the triangular tip.

Macramé Bag:

To Make the Handle:

This lash may look intimidating, but as a general rule it's really only one underhand knot type that's done a couple of different ways. Read on, and wait! We'll begin by hitching the bag tie. You would need to tie each half of the tie individually, so the length of each bit of string will be half the length of the tie as a whole. Our lashes were to be a total of 45cm (18"') as a guide, so the string pieces we cut were half that case. Create the string into equal parts and tie it to the collapsed end of your band.

Complete four knots. Beginning with the knot on the right, take the inward string and circle it around the external string. Fix the knot and this is what it ought to resemble. Rehash the past knot, just using the following string this time. This is one side of the knots done. Knot the opposite side of the ties using the equivalent hitching strategy, just turning around the course this time. This is the two sides done. Rehash this for the two sides multiple times. Once more, using the equivalent tying technique, interface the two strands by broadening the knots. This is what the expanding line resembles.

Rehash these all-inclusive lines multiple times. At that point alter the course and knot from left to directly for the following 3 lines. At that point rehash the side knots. When you've done this, you have completed a large portion of the tie! Rehash this for the other lash and band, we'll associate them later on. To polish off the knotwork, rehash a similar knot.

Clip off one of the strands in the knot, at that point proceed with the tying another knot using the following strand. This is what the completed end will resemble. To join the lashes together, line up the closures and sew together with needle and string. To make the body of the rope pack, cut 10 bits of string that are multiple times the ideal length of your bag.

As a reference, the pack we made is 15" (38cm). Knot it onto the gold band using the collapsed end like previously. The body of the rope pack will be ended with box ties. Taking two strings as an afterthought, circle it around the two center strands. Rehash the knot, and pull the knot tight. Rehash the knots on the remainder of the strands, make sure to keep the separations between the knots and the bands the equivalent. We did our own 3" down from the circle.

Keep doing box knots for the subsequent column, just using the strings one strand over this time. Knot 3 columns of box knots on the two sides, before tying the sides of the bag by using two strands from either side. Keep doing box knots until the pack is the size you are after. Cut off the parts of the bargains in the event that you don't need any tuft ends, and put a touch of paste into the knots to make sure about them. Flip the pack out.

Conclusion

Thank you for making it to the end. The beauty of Macramé as a vintage art that has survived extinction for centuries and has continued to thrive as a technique of choice for making simple but sophisticated items is simply unrivalled. The simple fact that you have decided to read this manual means that you are well on your way to making something great. There is truly a certain, unequaled feeling of satisfaction that comes from crafting your own masterpiece.

The most important rule in Macramé is the maxim: "Practice makes perfect." If you cease to practice constantly, your skills are likely to deteriorate over time. So, keep your skills sharp, exercise the creative parts of your brain, and keep creating mind-blowing handmade masterpieces. Jewelry and fashion accessories made with even the most basic Macramé's are always a beauty to behold, hence they serve as perfect gifts for loved ones on special occasions. Presenting a Macramé bracelet to someone, for instance passes the message that you didn't just remember to get them a gift, you also treasure them so much that you chose to invest your time into crafting something unique specially for them too, and trust me, that is a very powerful message. However, the most beautiful thing about Macramé is perhaps the fact that it helps to create durable items. Hence you can keep a piece of decoration, or a fashion accessory you made for yourself for many years, enjoy the value and still feel nostalgic anytime you remember when you made it. It even feels better when you made that item with someone. This feature of durability also makes Macramé accessories incredibly perfect gifts.

Presenting a Macramé bracelet to someone, for instance passes the message that you didn't just remember to get them a gift, you also treasure them so much that you chose to invest your time into crafting something unique specially for them too, and trust me, that is a very powerful message. However, the most beautiful thing about Macramé is perhaps the fact that it helps to create durable items. Hence you can keep a piece of decoration, or a fashion accessory you made for yourself for many years, enjoy the value and still feel nostalgic anytime you remember when you made it. It even feels better when you made that item with someone. This feature of durability also makes Macramé accessories incredibly perfect gifts.

Macramé can also serve as an avenue for you to begin your dream small business. After perfecting your Macramé skills, you can conveniently sell your items and get paid well for your products, especially if you can perfectly make items like bracelets that people buy a lot. You could even train people and start your own little company that makes bespoke Macramé fashion accessories. The opportunities that Macramé presents are truly endless.

Remember that Macramé has proven to be an excellent natural treatment for those undergoing recovery procedures and helps to restore memories once again, making it a unique experience for all. Playing with and tying the ropes, strengthens arms and hands, which helps relax wrist and finger joints. It also helps to calm the mind and soul, as attention is necessary, and the repeated patterns put the weaver in a meditative mood. It is believed that stress is reduced by the fingertips, making macramé knotting a calming task.

As a result of the creativity that goes into macramé's macramé ting, a lot of people enjoy doing it for a craft, in fact, some people believe that macramé is a natural therapy to improve mental abilities, strengthen arms and joints, improve concentration and calm the mind. This, however, does not imply that no great artistic skill is required. It is necessary to use macramé to be in a meditative mood and carefully weave leather into macramé s and cords.

Macramé can also be used in a number of home and fashion products. Bags, clothing, shoes, jewelry, door hangers, hanging baskets and plant hangers can be decorated with this classic braiding.

I hope you have learned something!

Printed in Great Britain
by Amazon

59254480R00070